# CODING
# KIDS IN C++

CW01457466

# Table of Contents

# Disclaimer

# Free Gift

We do want you to succeed in coding. To ensure your success, we are giving you a free list of projects that you can work on once you are completed with this book.

https://coding.gr8.com/

# Introduction

## What is Programming

Programming is the art of writing a computer program. A computer program is a set of instructions that a machine can comprehend to perform a certain task. Computer programming is how humans communicate with machines.

Computers are pretty good at following the instructions we give them.

A program is just simply a list of steps that should be followed to achieve a goal. It is just like a recipe, to prepare your favorite dish you just need to follow the instructions on the recipe.

The only issue is that computers do not speak English as we do, they speak their own language. This computer language is known as machine language.

There is a part on the computer called the interpreter, which interprets our instructions to machine language so that the computer is able to understand the instructions we are giving it. This interpreter is also known as a **compiler.**

A compiler is the interface between the programming language and the machine. A programming language is a very simple language to learn and there are numerous programming languages out there. We are only going to learn C++ in this book.

As you know, spoken languages usually have grammar. Grammar is a way of arranging words in a language to make sense to others who speak that language. Programming languages have grammar as well, which we call *syntax*.

In order for the compiler to understand you, you have to use the proper syntax or else it will cause an error. We will at first spend a lot of time learning the syntax of our programming language.

In summary, we write a program using a programming language. The programming languages communicates with the compiler. The compiler translates the language to machine language and then runs the program. The computer reads our instructions and does what we have told it to do.

Your first programming language is usually the toughest to learn but after learning it, it becomes easier to learn other languages.

# Why C++

You can do a lot after learning C++. You can make games, use the Arduino board to make cool projects or even program planes if you are allowed to do that. The only limit you have is your imagination.

The main benefit of C++ is that it is very portable between operating systems and compilers. This means that the same code can be used in Windows, Linux, Opera etc.

C++ has a large community support with developer forums, online tutorials, Facebook community groups, which is very significant for beginner programmers. It's much easier to learn as you can ask other people in the community if you get stuck.

C++ is also very scalable and flexible in multiple environments. This means that it can be used by beginner programmers and advanced professionals for different purposes. It can also be used to code games, applications, software and apps.

C++ is wildly used in graphics and is now used in emerging technologies like image processing, pattern recognition and in embedded systems like location tracing.

C++ is more efficient at using computer memory, so it saves space on your hard drive.

# Why Learn Programming

Programming at its core is not really about writing code but thinking of ways to solve problems. You get to learn and appreciate that there are different ways to tackle a problem and sometimes one way is better than the other. You also learn that breaking a big problem into small parts makes your work easier.

It is also about learning how to collaborate with others. People usually assume that programmers work by themselves to solve problems, but programmers act as a team most of the time. We like sharing what we have built with others, and this enables us to learn from one another there by advancing each other's skills.

In addition, programming teaches you to never give up easily, because your programs will never work out the first time you write them. You will get errors from time to time but as a programmer you don't let them bring you down. You pick yourself up when you fall and try again.

Finally, you feel comfortable in this digital world where computers run almost everything. To you it will not be magic as you know how to use computers to do your tasks.

At the end of the day even if you don't become a programmer, you will be able to know how computers can help you out in your work and gain all these skills.

# Setting Up the Workspace

In order to write code, you need at least a text editor and a compiler.

A text editor is just a program that enables you to write and save code as a file.

Files usually have extensions to their file names to indicate the kind of file it is. When writing
C++ files, the files will have the extension .cpp , example main.cpp

We are going to use an application known as Code::Blocks to write, compile and run our programs. Code::Blocks is what is known as an IDE , integrated development environment.

An IDE has everything you need to write, compile and run a program in one place.

Below is a picture of the layout of the Code::Blocks IDE

```cpp
#include <iostream>

using namespace std;

int main()
{
    cout << "Hello world!" << endl;
    return 0;
}
```

# Downloading and Installing Code::Blocks

You will need:

1. A laptop/ Desktop
2. Internet Connection
3. Web browser such as Chrome, Windows Edge or Firefox

Go to this website and download the Code::Blocks application:
https://www.fosshub.com/Code-Blocks.html?dwl=codeblocks-20.03mingw-setup.exe

Just copy and paste the link to the browser

Note: please ensure that you download the file named Code Blocks Windows 64 bit (including compiler).

This version includes the compiler which we need

After that just install the application and open it when done:

You can head over to the Code::Blocks website at the following link:
https://www.codeblocks.org/ to learn more about it. It also includes user manual and links to download the IDE for other operating systems

# Hello World in C++

The first program that all programmers write when learning a new programming language is known as Hello World.

It is just basically writing a program that displays the words 'Hello World' to the screen. Since we are programmers now, we say that we are *printing* the words 'Hello World' to the screen.

I will be giving out code examples, and you will have to type the examples in the Code::Blocks and click on the build and run button to compile and execute the code in order to see the results.

## Creating A Project in Code::Blocks

In order to run code in Code::Blocks we have to first create a project. So first of all we need to open up Code::Blocks.

To create a project, click on **File > New > Project**

In the pop-up window select **Console application** and click on the button **Go**

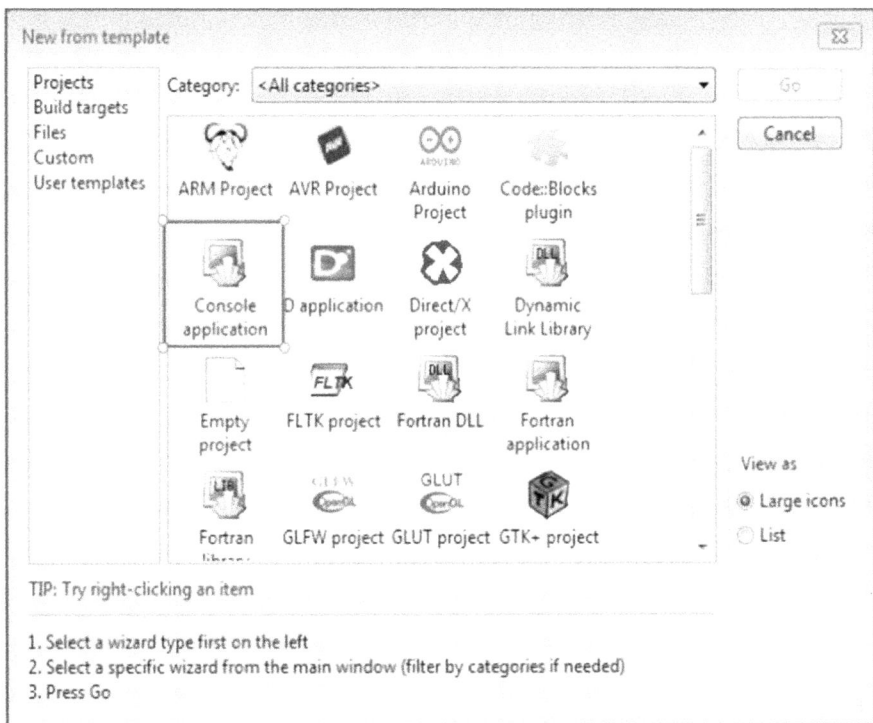

**New from template**

| Projects | Category: <All categories> | | Go |
| Build targets | | | |
| Files | | | Cancel |
| Custom | | | |
| User templates | | | |

ARM Project   AVR Project   Arduino Project   Code::Blocks plugin

Console application   D application   Direct/X project   Dynamic Link Library

Empty project   FLTK project   Fortran DLL   Fortran application

Fortran library   GLFW project   GLUT project   GTK+ project

View as
◉ Large icons
○ List

TIP: Try right-clicking an item

1. Select a wizard type first on the left
2. Select a specific wizard from the main window (filter by categories if needed)
3. Press Go

Ensure you select **C++** in this window
Click **Next** on the information window

Give the Project a title, for now it is **Hello World**. Select which folder it will be saved at.

---

Console application                                            [ ⊠ ]

**Console**

Please select the folder where you want the new project to be created as well as its title.

Project title:

Hello World

Folder to create project in:

C:\Users\asaria\Documents\cpp_projects\   [ ... ]

Project filename:

Hello World.cbp

Resulting filename:

C:\Users\asaria\Documents\cpp_projects\Hello Worlc

[ < Back ]    [ Next > ]    [ Cancel ]

---

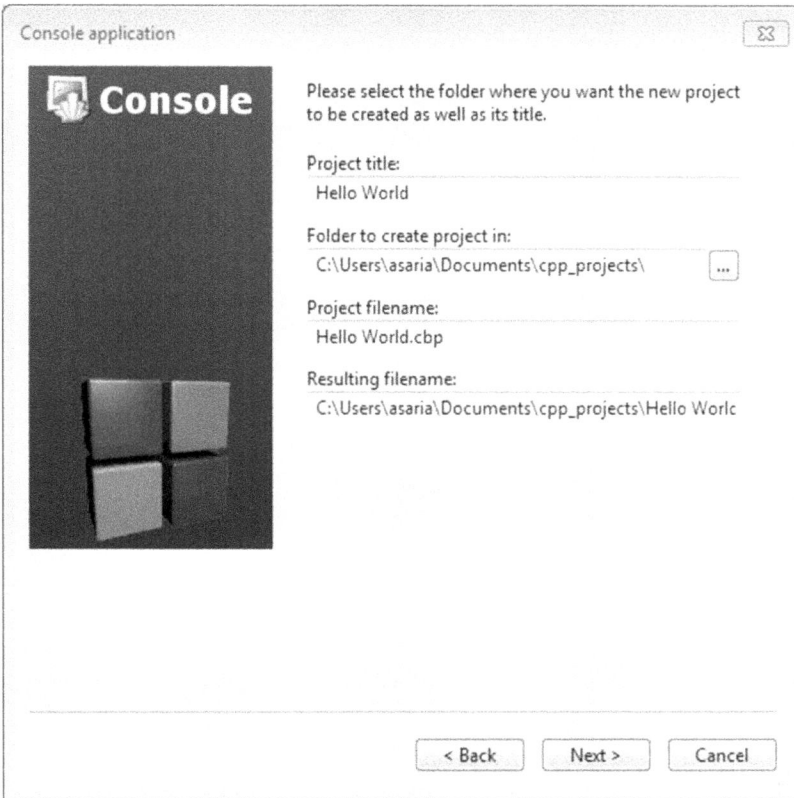

Ensure that you have **GNU GCC Compiler** selected as the compiler and click on **Finish.**

Now on the left-hand side, under Hello World, click on the **+** icon next to the **Sources folder** to reveal the **main.cpp** file. Double click on it to display the file on the editor window on the right-hand side.

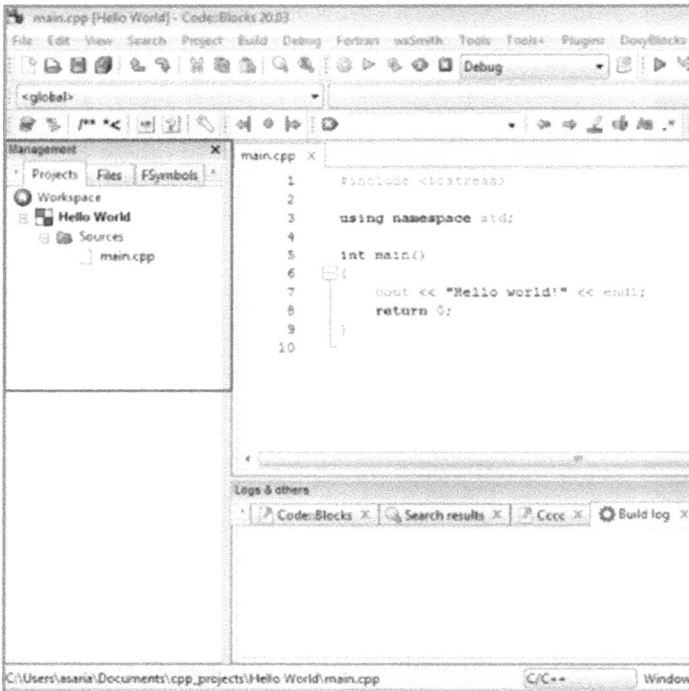

The code in the editor looks like the example below

## Code

```
#include <iostream>
  using namespace std;

int main()
{

    cout << "Hello World" << endl;

    return 0;
```

}

I am pretty sure that the above code looks overwhelming when you first see it. But we are going to understand what it all means by the end of a few chapters. For now hang in there as I try to explain the main part of this program.
The trick with programming is to persevere as things get easier the more you learn.

Let's first run the code.

## Running the code

To run the code, we have to compile it first.

In Code::Blocks, we use the term *build* instead of compile. This is because a project usually consists of multiple C++ files and we call the process of compiling all of them building.

There are three buttons on top of the editor that enable us to build and run our project.

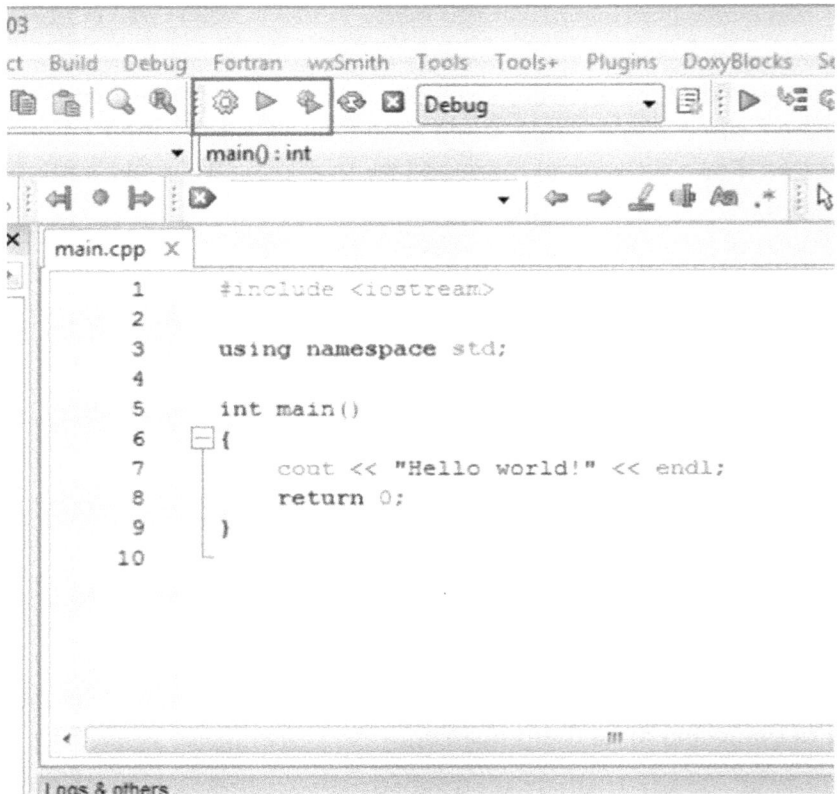

```
03
ct  Build  Debug  Fortran  wxSmith  Tools  Tools+  Plugins  DoxyBlocks  S

                                          Debug

                              main() : int

main.cpp  X
        1         #include <iostream>
        2
        3         using namespace std;
        4
        5         int main()
        6         {
        7             cout << "Hello world!" << endl;
        8             return 0;
        9         }
       10

Logs & others
```

The yellow gear button enables you to build the project, the green play button enables you to run the build project, while the third, which is a combination of the gear and play button, enables you to build and run the project. Click on the combination of the two to execute the project.

A pop-up window will appear with the words 'Hello World' as shown below.

```
C:\Users\asaria\Documents\cpp_projects\s\bin\Debug\s.exe
Hello world!

Process returned 0 (0x0)   execution time : 0.014 s
Press any key to continue.
```

This is what is known as the **console** or **terminal**. The console shows the output in C++. Just close the window to get rid of it.

NOTE: make sure that you save you file before building and running it, this can be done by pressing **Control-s (Ctrl+s)** after every change

# Explanation of the code

The main line in this program, is the line:

cout << "Hello World" << endl;
`

First of all, notice that the line ends with a semicolon (;), this is very important as it indicates the end of this instruction.

**cout** is just the programmer way of calling a screen, you can think of it as the short form of console output.

The symbols **<<** just mean display the things after me on the screen

'Hello World' is the text that we want to display on the screen. Notice that it is surrounded by double quotes. The double quotes are part of the syntax and are very important.

We call text surrounded by double quotes a *string.*

The next << symbol over means, add what's after me to the text 'Hello world'. In programming we call this **concatenation** that is adding two strings together

**endl**, means add a newline, a newline is just like pressing enter while typing something on the computer, it takes you to a next line below the current text

As you can see when writing programs, we do not just write it in plain English, we follow some specific rules known as the *syntax* of the language.

# Exercise

1. Change the text so that the program prints out your name, build and run the code.

2. Write the line of code **cout << "Hello World";** two times and see what is printed on the console. How is that different from writing **cout << 'Hello World' << endl;** two times

 3. Create a new project and give it any name you like and store it in a different folder location.

>   a. For this new project click the run icon and notice what happens

>   b. For this new project click the build gear icon then the run icon individually and note what happens.

# Variables

In this chapter I will first take you through the main parts of the computer that are important in programming.

The main part of the computer is known as the processor. This is what actually reads your code and does what you instructed.

In addition, there is a storage area known as **RAM**, which stands for **Random Access Memory**. This is where everything you need is stored, even your program is stored here.

You can think of it as a bunch of shelves with boxes where you can store things. In addition, these boxes are of different sizes and type. Hence you can determine what you can store in them.

In addition, we can label these boxes so that we can refer to the name later easily.

## Variable Assignment

A variable is a name given to a value that is stored in memory.

A variable name is also known as an **identifier.**

You can think of a variable as a box where we place our value in, and a variable name as a label we place on the box.

There is also a thing called data type assigned to each box. A data type is a type of information that is stored in a box. That means that the particular variable can store only a particular type of data. Examples of data types include strings, numbers, booleans etc.

Below is an example of a variable assignment. We write it in Code::Blocks in a new project called variables, save the file by pressing **Control-S** then build and run.

## Example code

```
main.cpp  X
 1     #include <iostream>
 2         using namespace std;
 3
 4    □  int main() {
 5
 6             int radius = 20;
 7             cout << radius << endl;
 8                radius = 40;
 9            cout << radius << endl;
10             return 0;
11     └   }
12
13
```

Above we have declared a variable of the name *radius* of data type int, meaning integer and initialized it to the value 20.

**int** is what we call the **data type**. Using the box analogy a data type determines the type of the box to store our value. The value which we store is 20. The variable name is called **radius**, which means the label on the box is radius.

The value of the variable can change throughout the program as long as it is of the same data type. In the above program, we change the value to 40.

This is acceptable as 40 is an int (integer) data type.

## Data types

Below is a list of data types available and the kind and range of values they represent. Each data type has an example associated with it.

### int

The data type **int** stands for integer. An integer is a whole number, meaning that it cannot have a decimal to it. Examples of integers are 1,0,45,768,23343 etc.

Example: int radius = 2;

# long

The data type **long** is also a whole number, but the numbers used can be a lot bigger than int. long variables can hold up to 20 digits, while in variables can only hold 10 digits.
For example, below, **x**, **y** and **result** are long variables that can hold numbers up to 20 digits.

main.cpp X

```
1    #include<iostream>
2    using namespace std;
3
4    int main(){
5        long x = 9988891919;
6        long y = 3465829;
7        long result = x * y;
8        cout << result;
9        return 0;
10   }
11
```

# float

Represent numbers with decimals places. See example below. pi is a float variable with a value of 3.142 and areaofcircle is another float variable.

```cpp
#include<iostream>
using namespace std;

int main(){
    float pi = 3.142;
    int radius = 3;
    float areaOfCircle = pi * radius * radius;
    cout << areaOfCircle;
    return 0;
}
```

```
C:\Users\asaria\Documents\cpp_projects\Variables\bin\Debug\Variables.exe
28.278
Process returned 0 (0x0)   execution time : 0.034 s
Press any key to continue.
```

# double

A double variable can hold numbers that contain decimals places with higher precision and can hold more decimal places (up to 15 decimal places).
In below example, acceleration, mass and force are three double variables that can each hold numbers that contain up to 15 decimal places.

main.cpp X

```cpp
1    #include<iostream>
2    using namespace std;
3
4    int main(){
5        double acceleration = 9.98;
6        double mass = 30.03;
7        double force = acceleration * mass;
8        cout << force;
9        return 0;
10   }
```

```
C:\Users\asaria\Documents\cpp_projects\Variables\bin\Debug\Variables.exe
299.699
Process returned 0 (0x0)   execution time : 0.014 s
Press any key to continue.
```

# bool

It stands for boolean.
It can only hold two values, the value **true** or **false**.
The boolean variable is used for conditionals.
In the example below, two boolean variables **isHungry** and **isSleepy** are declared.
If **isHungry** is true, the program prints **"I am hungry"** on the screen.
If **isSleepy** is true, the program prints **"I am sleepy"** on the screen.

```cpp
main.cpp  X
1    #include<iostream>
2    using namespace std;
3
4    int main(){
5        bool isHungry = true;
6        bool isSleepy = false;
7        if(isHungry){
8            cout << "I am hungry" << endl;
9        }
10       if(isSleepy){
11           cout << "I am sleepy" << endl;
12       }
13
14       isSleepy = true;
15       if(isSleepy){
16           cout << "I am going to bed" << endl;
17       }
18
19       return 0;
20   }
```

■ C:\Users\asaria\Documents\cpp_projects\Variables\bin\Debug\Variables.exe

```
I am hungry
I am going to bed

Process returned 0 (0x0)   execution time : 0.015 s
Press any key to continue.
```

# char

char stands for character. char is a variable that can hold only one value. The value is a string of length 1. In below example, **excellent** is a char variable that holds the grade of a student in Mathematics.

```cpp
#include<iostream>
using namespace std;

int main(){
    char excellent = 'A';
    cout << "Congratulations you got an " << excellent << " in maths" << endl;
    return 0;
}
```

```
C:\Users\asaria\Documents\cpp_projects\Variables\bin\Debug\Variables.exe
Congratulations you got an A in maths

Process returned 0 (0x0)    execution time : 0.015 s
Press any key to continue.
```

# string

A string is a variable used to store text. It can hold a string of any length. In the below example, **yourName** is a variable that holds the value **"Catherine"**.

```cpp
#include<iostream>
using namespace std;

int main(){
    string yourName = "Catherine";
    cout << "Good morning  " << yourName << endl;
    return 0;
}
```

```
C:\Users\asaria\Documents\cpp_projects\Variables\bin\Debug\Variables.exe
Good morning  Catherine

Process returned 0 (0x0)   execution time : 0.041 s
Press any key to continue.
```

# Variable names

A C++ variable name must start with either a letter or an underscore and all the rest of the characters must be letters, digits or an underscore.

Examples of valid variable names are:

```
x
x1
x_1_abc
RATE
bigBonus_
```

Examples of invalid variable names:

```
 12
3x
%change data
-1 PROG.CPP
```

The first three, 12 3x %change, are not allowed because they do not start with a letter or an underscore.

C++ is also case sensitive, meaning that the following are three distinct variable names:

```
Rate
RATE
Rate
```

## Camel Case

Camel case is a programming practice where multiple words are written without spaces and the first letter of each word is capitalized (except for the first word)

The word *end of car* would become: endOfCar
Camel case is a commonly used programming practice to name variables.

## Keywords

Keywords are names that cannot be used as variable names as they are reserved for programming language syntax.

If you use them as variable names the compiler will throw errors, or you might end up changing the basic functionality of some basic function.

Examples of keywords include the basic data types, such as int, bool and the rest, and names such as struct and class.

## Comments

Sometimes we want to explain our code so that others can understand what we did. In the future that information will help us remember what we did as we go through the code.

In programming we achieve this by writing comments within our code. There are two types of comments, single line comments and multiline comments.

Single line comments begin with two forward slashes (*//*) while multiline comments sit in between the following symbols: */\*\*/*

Examples of comments:

// Test Code

/* Line 1 of Comments
Line 2 of Comments */

## Declaring variables

All variables must be declared or defined before they are used.

To declare/define a variable you just need to specify a data type and a variable name followed by a semicolon:

When you declare a variable without giving it a value, we say that the variable is *uninitialized.*
Uninitialized variable will have a random value in it.

Giving an uninitialized variable a value is known as *initializing* it.

You can also declare and initialize a variable at the same time.

In this example we are going to make use of comments and declare some variables whose value we will print to the console

Create a new project in Code::Blocks, write the following code, build and run it.

# Example code

```cpp
#include <iostream>
using namespace std;

int main() {

/*
    This is a multiline comment
    As can be seen , it spans
    multiple lines
*/
    int length; // declaring the variable length
    int width; // declaring the variable width

    length = 20; // initializing the variable len
    width = 20;// initializing the variable width

    int depth = 40; // declaring and initializing

    cout << length << endl;
    cout << width << endl;
    cout << depth << endl;

    return 0;
}
```

# Explanation

In the above program, in the main block of code, we first begin by
writing a multiline comment by writing in between /**/.
We then declare two variables of type int which are *length* and *width*
without initializing them, which we do later.

We then declare and initialize the variable *depth* of type int to 40.
Finally, we print the values of length, width and depth to the console
each on its own separate line.

# Exercise

1. Write a program that contains statements that output the values of five or six variables that have been defined, but not initialized. Compile and run the program. What is the output? Explain.
2. Create a string variable with your name and print it to the console.
3. Create a char variable and print it to the console
4. Create a bool variable and print it to the console
5. Create a float variable and print it to the console
6. Create a long variable named, time of day, in camel case and print it to the console

# Mathematics Operations

In this section we will make a small calculator that only performs multiplication of two numbers. The program will ask us for two numbers to multiply and print the result of multiplication.

First, we will go through how to perform mathematic operations in C++

## Addition

Addition is done using the + operator

## Addition Example code

```
main.cpp X

1       #include<iostream>
2       using namespace std;
3
4       int main(){
5
6           int x = 1;
7           int y = 2;
8           int sum = x + y ;
9           cout << sum ;
10          return 0;
11      }
```

The output of the code will be **3**, which is the sum of x and y.

# Subtraction

Subtraction is done using the - operator

## Subtraction Example code

main.cpp  X

```cpp
1    #include<iostream>
2    using namespace std;
3
4    int main(){
5
6        int x = 1;
7        int y = 2;
8        int difference = x - y ;
9        cout << difference ;
10       return 0;
11   }
12
```

The output of the code will be **-1**

# Multiplication

Multiplication is done using the * operator

## Multiplication Example code

```
main.cpp  X
1        #include<iostream>
2        using namespace std;
3
4      int main(){
5
6            int x = 3;
7            int y = 2;
8            int multiplication = x * y ;
9            cout << multiplication ;
10           return 0;
11     }
12
```

The output of the code will be **6**

# Division

Division is done using the / operator, this returns the quotient of the division

## Division Example code

main.cpp ✕

```
1              #include<iostream>
2         using namespace std;
3
4    int main(){
5
6             int x = 3;
7             int y = 2;
8             int quotient = x / y ;
9             cout << quotient ;
10            return 0;
11        }
12
```

The output of above code will be 1.5

# Remainder

In order to get the remainder of a division use the modulo operator which is represented by the symbol **%**.

```
main.cpp ×
1
2      #include<iostream>
3      using namespace std;
4
5      int main(){
6
7          int x = 3;
8          int y = 2;
9          int remainder = x % y ;
10         cout << remainder ;
11         return 0;
12      }
13
```

The output of the code will be **1**, which is the reminder when x is divided by y.

# Getting Input from users

So far, we have just been printing things to the console without any input from the user. In this section we are going to make our program more exciting by asking for input from users.

## cin

**cin** is use to accept input from the keyboard, it can be thought of as standing for console input

# Example code

```
main.cpp  X
1    #include <iostream>
2      using namespace std;
3
4    int main() {
5        int num;
6
7        cout << "Enter a number: ";
8
9        // take integer input
10       cin >> num;
11
12       cout << "You entered: " << num;
13
14       return 0;
15   }
16
```

## Explanation

Here we first create a variable called *num* of type int which we will use to store the value we get from the keyboard input.

We the ask the user for some input, and just print it back to the console: 'You entered: 1', if you type in 1 in the console

# A simple calculator

We will have to ask the user for two numbers to multiply, and the show the result of multiplication to the user.

## Example Code

```cpp
main.cpp  X
 1    #include <iostream>
 2       using namespace std;
 3
 4    int main() {
 5          int num1;
 6          int num2;
 7
 8          // prompt to enter num1
 9          cout << "Enter a num1: ";
10
11          cin >> num1;
12
13          // prompt to enter num2
14          cout << "Enter a num2: ";
15
16          cin >> num2;
17
18
19          int multiplication = num1 * num2;
20          cout << "Result of multiplication:  " << multiplication;
21
22          return 0;
23    }
24
```

# Explanation

We first declare two int type variables that will store the use input that is num1 and num2

We prompt the user for num1, then store it in the corresponding variable using cin. We do the same to num2

We then perform multiplication on the two and display the result to the user

# Exercise

1.  Convert each of the following mathematical formulas to a C++ expression, each variable getting its value from the user input
    1.  3x
    2.  3x + y
    3.  (x + y)/7
    4.  (3x + y) / (z + 2)

2. Write a program that takes in school marks in 6 subjects using 6 input variables. Calculate total marks and average marks for the subjects
3. Write a program that takes in a integer from the user and determines whether it is an even number or an odd number. Hint: Use modulo

# Functions

A function is a group of lines of code that perform a given task. Each function has been assigned a name and will be referenced by that name in the program.

In C++ functions are expected to return a value and the data type of the value to be returned is usually indicated when defining a function.

In this section we will write a function that calculates the area of a rectangle

## Example of a function

The area of a rectangle is equal to its length multiplied by width, so below is a function to calculate it

Write this before the main function as so:

```
main.cpp  X
  1        #include <iostream>
  2        using namespace std;
  3
  4        //defining the function named areaOfRectangle
  5        int areaOfRectangle( int length , int width){
  6            int area = length * width;
  7            return area;
  8        }
  9
 10        int main() {
 11
 12            return 0; |
 13        }
 14
 15
 16
```

## Explanation

*int* is the data type of the value to be returned, so we expect the function to give us back an integer when we run it. This is indicated by the line *return area;* just above the closing curly brace in line 7. Notice the variable *area* is declared as an integer type since that is the variable that the function returns.

*areaOfRectangle* is the name we give to our function. Notice that it is written in camel case.

What follows the name of a function is a pair of parentheses, in the parenthesis we declare two variables, and these variables are known as **parameters.** In the example above, **length** and **width** are the parameters.

They will hold values we pass to the function when we run it and they can be accessed with the function's block of code.

We then have our code in curly braces so as to mark it as the lines of code associated with that function name.

Finally, we have the **return** statement.

# Running a function

Look at the code below

```
main.cpp  X
1    #include <iostream>
2    using namespace std;
3
4    int areaOfRectangle( int length , int width){
5        int area = length * width;
6        return area;
7    }
8    int main() {
9
10       // calling the areaOfRectangle function
11       // length = 4 and width = 5
12
13       int area = areaOfRectangle(4,5);
14
15       cout << "Area is: " << area << endl;
16       return 0;
17   }
18
```

```
C:\Users\asaria\Documents\cpp_projects\Functions\bin\Debug\Functions.exe
Area is: 20

Process returned 0 (0x0)   execution time : 0.061 s
Press any key to continue.
```

## Explanation

When we want to run a function, we usually say that we are **calling** that function.

Some functions take in values when there are being called like ours does, we call these values *arguments* of the function.

Notice the syntax used to pass arguments to functions, we first write the function name and in between an opening and closing parenthesis we write the arguments, separated by commas.

So, in our example, we are calling the function *areaOfRectangle* passing in the two arguments, that is, 4 and 5.

We expect the function to return a value, which is the area that has been calculated and the value of the area calculated to be of the data type integer.

For this reason, we assign the returned value to the variable named *area* of type i*nt*.

We then print the result to the screen. In this case, the area of the rectangle is 20 so that is the output shown on the screen.

## Void Functions

The functions known as void functions are functions that do not return anything after being called

# Example code

```cpp
#include <iostream>
using namespace std;

void showResults(double fDegrees, double cDegrees){
    cout << fDegrees
    << " degrees Fahrenheit is equivalent to\n"
    << cDegrees << " degrees Celsius.\n";
}

int main() {
    showResults(30.03, 100.5);
    return 0;
}
```

```
C:\Users\asaria\Documents\cpp_projects\Functions\bin\Debug\Functions.exe
30.03 degrees Fahrenheit is equivalent to
100.5 degrees Celsius.

Process returned 0 (0x0)   execution time : 0.079 s
Press any key to continue.
```

## Explanation

Notice that the specified return type is void and that we do not use the return keyword in the body of the function.

Apart from that there are not any other differences with the way we define other non-void functions.

## Exercise

1. Create a function called Descending() that takes four arguments. Each argument is a number of type int. The function returns true if the four numbers are in descending order; otherwise, it returns false. For example, Descending(4, 3, 3, 1) and Descending(3, 2, 2, 1) both return true, whereas Descending(2, 1, 3, 2) returns false.

2. Create a function called isOdd()that takes in one argument of type int and returns a Boolean value. The function returns true if the input is an odd number. It returns false if it is an even number.

3. What is the output of the following program?

```cpp
#include <iostream>
using namespace std;
void sayhi();
void hide(int audiencenumber);
int main()
{
        sayhi();
        hide(6);
        cout << "Extra time:\n";
        hide(2);
        sayhi();
```

```
        cout << "End of program.\n";
        return 0;
}
void sayhi()
{
        cout << "Hello\n";
}
void hide(int audiencenumber)
{
        if (audiencenumber < 5)
        return;
        cout << "Bye\n";
}
```

4. Write a function that calculates the perimeter of a circle, that has a parameter called radius of type int and returns type double. Use pi as a double variable of value 3.142.

# Conditional Statement

We usually want to do something only when a certain condition is true. For example, if it is sunny outside then we go out and play, else we stay at home.

The statement, it is sunny outside, can only either be true or false.

In programming we have a data type that can only store the value true or false, this data type is known as a **boolean**. In C++ we usually shorten it to **bool**.

In addition, we sometimes want to run lines of code only when a certain condition is true, and we achieve this using **if** statement. Let's do an example, which will make it easier to understand

## Example Code

```
Build  Debug  Fortran  wxSmith  Tools  Tools+  Plugins  DoxyBlocks  Settings  Help
                                    Debug

                main() : int

main.cpp  X
     1      #include<iostream>
     2      using namespace std;
     3
     4      int main(){
     5          bool sunny = true;
     6
     7          if(sunny){
     8              cout << "You can go outside to play" << endl;
     9          }else{
    10              cout << "Don't go outside to play" << endl;
    11          }
    12
    13          return 0;
    14      }
    15
```

## Explanation

In the above example, we first create a variable called *sunny* that holds a boolean value since it has the data type *bool.*

Using the *if* statement we check whether it is true that it is sunny, if it is, we print "You can go outside to play" to the screen else we print "Don't go outside to play"

## Exercise

Change the variable *sunny* to be *false* and see what will be printed.

# Comparison Operators

Comparison operators compare two values and return either true or false

Examples of comparison operators are:

**Less than (<)**
It returns true if the value on the left is less than the value on the right. Otherwise, it returns false.

**Greater than (>)**
It returns true if the value on the left is greater than the value on the right. Otherwise, it returns false.

**Less than or equal to (<=)**
It returns true if the value on the left is less than or equal to the value on the right. Otherwise, it returns false.

**Greater than or equal to (>=)**
It returns true if the value on the left is greater than or equal to the value on the right. Otherwise, it returns false.

**Equal to (==)**
It returns true if the value on the left is equal to the value on the right. Otherwise, it returns false.

**Not equal to (!=)**
It returns true if the value on the left is not equal to the value on the right. Otherwise, it returns false.

# Example of use of comparison operators

Let's say you want to print to the screen the string 'x is greater than 5' if x is indeed greater than 5 else you print 'x is less than or equal to 5'

```
main.cpp X
1    #include<iostream>
2    using namespace std;
3
4    int main(){
5        int x = 3;
6
7        if(x > 5){
8            cout << "x is greater than 5" << endl;
9        }else{
10           cout << "x is less than or equal to 5" << endl;
11       }
12       return 0;
13   }
```

```
"C:\Users\asaria\Documents\cpp_projects\Conditional Statements\bin\Debug\Conditional Stateme...
x is less than or equal to 5

Process returned 0 (0x0)    execution time : 0.021 s
Press any key to continue.
```

# Building Boolean Expressions

A **Boolean expression** is any expression that has one of two values. It is either true or false. It is basically an expression that compares two values and returns true/false.

Two comparisons can be combined using the "and" operator, which is **&&** in C++. For example, the following Boolean expression is true provided a is bigger in value than 5 and a is smaller than 10:

**(5 < a) && (a < 10)**

The above operation returns true if a is between 5 and 10 (not including 5,10).

When two comparisons are connected using a **&&**, the entire expression is true, provided both comparisons are true; otherwise, the entire expression is false.

You can also combine two comparisons using the "or" operator, which is spelled **||** in C++. For example, the following is true provided b is less than 2 or b is greater than 9:

**(b < 2) || (b > 9)**

The above expression returns true if b is less than 2 or b is greater than 9.

In an expression that uses || operation, the expression is true provided that either of the comparisons is true. If both expressions are false, then the expression is false.

A Boolean expression can be negated using the ! operation. For example,

**!(a > b)**
Returns true if "a is not greater than b".

In most cases, there is no need to use the exclamation (!) operator.

For example,
**!(a > b) is the same as to a <= b**

# Truth Tables

The following are known as truth tables. It indicates all the possibilities that a combination of each expression can be and the resulting boolean value.

AND

| expression1 | expression2 | expression1 && expression2 |
| --- | --- | --- |
| true | True | True |
| true | False | False |
| false | True | False |
| false | False | False |

OR

| expression1 | expression2 | expression1 \|\| expression2 |
| --- | --- | --- |
| true | True | True |
| true | False | True |
| false | True | True |
| false | False | False |

NOT

| expression | ! expression |
|------------|--------------|
| true | False |
| false | True |

# Example of Boolean expressions

Let's say that you only buy food when you are hungry, and you have money. To represent this in code it will be something like this.

Example

main.cpp  X

```cpp
1    #include<iostream>
2    using namespace std;
3
4
5    int main(){
6
7        bool isHungry = true;
8        bool hasMoney = true;
9
10       if( isHungry && hasMoney){
11           cout << "I will buy food" << endl;
12       }else{
13           cout << "I can't but  food" << endl;
14       }
15
16       return 0;
```

```
I will buy food

Process returned 0 (0x0)   execution time : 0.014 s
Press any key to continue.
```

## Explanation

The string 'I will buy food' only gets printed when the variables
**isHungry** and **hasMoney** are true. Otherwise, the string 'I can't buy
food' is printed.
Change the program to print 'I will buy food' if **isHungry** is true or
**hasMoney** is true.

## Exercise

1. Write a program that outputs the word **Small** if the score is less
   than 10 and **Big** if the value of the score is bigger than 100.

2. Write a program that outputs the word **Success** provided the
   variable **test** is greater than or equal to 50 and the value of the
   variable **codingPrograms** is greater than 5. Otherwise, the
   programs output the word **failure**. The variables **test** and
   **codingPrograms** are both of type int.

3. Write a program that outputs the word **Danger** if the variable
   **temp** is greater than 37, or the value of the variable **press** is

greater than 1, or both. Otherwise, the program prints the word **Great**. The variables **temp** and **press** are both of type int.

# Loops

Loops enable us to repeat a set of instructions a fixed number of times. It can also be repeated forever if we wanted to.

There are usually two types of loops, *finite loops* and *infinite loops*.

Finite loops repeat the set of instructions a countable number of times while infinite loops repeat a set of instructions forever.

## How we specify loops

In C++ there are two ways of declaring loops.
One way is to use the **for** keyword and the other is to use the **while** keyword.

### For loops

Let's say you want to print out your name 10 times to the console, you might think of writing out the instruction *'cout << "My name"<< endl;'* 10 times.
Using For loops is a good way to prevent repetition of the same statement and shorten the code.

# Example

## Explanation

To use the **for loop** we specify the number of times we want to run the block of code associated with that for loop.

The block of code associated with the for loop is in between the opening and closing curly braces
{
}

In our code the associated block of code has only the line: cout << "My name" << endl;

Inside the opening and closing parenthesis associated with the *for* keyword we specify three important things separated by two semicolons

The first is what number to begin counting at, for us, we begin counting from 1 so we declare the integer variable **i** holding the value 1.

The second, separated from the first by a semicolon, is the condition that should be true in order for the block of code associated with for loop to be executed. We usually use comparison operators such as >, <, <=, >= in this section.

In our case , **i <= 10**, means only run the block of code if the value of the variable i is less or equal to 10, otherwise stop the loop and proceed with the rest of the program.

Finally, the third part, separated by a semicolon from the second part, increments the count variable, in our case we increment by 1 using the special notation **i++**

In addition, this increment occurs after the block of code runs

## Exercise

1. Change the program to loop over our text 100 times

## Example Using Counter Inside Loop

We can use our declared integer inside the associated block of code, for example, we could print the value 1 to 10 with the code below.

```cpp
main.cpp  X

1    #include<iostream>
2    using namespace std;
3
4    int main(){
5
6
7        for(int i = 1 ; i <= 10; i++){
8            cout << i << endl;
9        }
10
11   return 0;
12   }
13
```

```
C:\Users\asaria\Documents\cpp_projects\Loops\bin\Debug\Loops.exe
1
2
3
4
5
6
7
8
9
10

Process returned 0 (0x0)   execution time : 0.026 s
Press any key to continue.
```

## while loops

**while** loops are similar to *for* loops, with the only difference being that it is only the condition to be met that is in the parenthesis associated with the while keyword.

## Example

```cpp
main.cpp  X
1     #include<iostream>
2     using namespace std;
3
4     int main(){
5
6         int i = 1;
7
8         while( i <= 10){
9             cout << "Hi from the while loop"<< endl;
10            i++;
11        }
12
13        return 0;
14    }
15
```

## Explanation

We first declare where we will start counting from in the line: **int i = 1;**

**while(i <= 10)**, means while the value of the variable *i* is less or equal to 10 run the associated block of code.

Notice that just before the closing brace we increment the value of i by 1.

The while loop then repeats to check whether i is less or equal to 10, if it is, it executes the associated block of code. If i is greater than 10, the block of code is not executed, and the program goes to the next instructions

# Infinite loops

Infinite loops occur when the condition that *for* loop or *while* loop checks in order to decide whether to run their associated block of code, is always **true**.
**So, it basically runs forever.**

## Example

```cpp
main.cpp  X

1    #include<iostream>
2    using namespace std;
3
4    int main(){
5
6
7        while( true ){
8            cout << "Hi from the infinite while loop"<< endl;
9
10       }
11
12       return 0;
13    }
14
```

C:\Users\asaria\Documents\cpp_projects\Loops\bin\Debug\Loops.exe

```
Hi from the infinite while loop
Hi from the infinite while loop
Hi from the infinite while loop
Hi from the infinite while loop
Hi from the infinite while loop
Hi from the infinite while loop
Hi from the infinite while loop
Hi from the infinite while loop
Hi from the infinite while loop
Hi from the infinite while loop
Hi from the infinite while loop
Hi from the infinite while loop
Hi from the infinite while loop
Hi from the infinite while loop
Hi from the infinite while loop
Hi from the infinite while loop
Hi from the infinite while loop
Hi from the infinite while loop
Hi from the infinite while loop
Hi from the infinite while loop
Hi from the infinite while loop
Hi from the infinite while loop
Hi from the infinite while loop
Hi from the infinite while loop
```

# Explanation

This will run forever as the condition is always true

# Infinite For Loop

An infinite for loop is defined as shown below:

```cpp
#include<iostream>
using namespace std;

int main(){


    for(;;){
        cout << "Hi from the infinite for loop"<< endl;

    }


    return 0;
}
```

C:\Users\asaria\Documents\cpp_projects\Loops\bin\Debug\Loops.exe

```
Hi from the infinite for loop
Hi from the infinite for loop
Hi from the infinite for loop
Hi from the infinite for loop
Hi from the infinite for loop
Hi from the infinite for loop
Hi from the infinite for loop
Hi from the infinite for loop
Hi from the infinite for loop
Hi from the infinite for loop
Hi from the infinite for loop
Hi from the infinite for loop
Hi from the infinite for loop
Hi from the infinite for loop
Hi from the infinite for loop
Hi from the infinite for loop
Hi from the infinite for loop
Hi from the infinite for loop
Hi from the infinite for loop
Hi from the infinite for loop
Hi from the infinite for loop
Hi from the infinite for loop
Hi from the infinite for loop
Hi from the infinite for loop
```

**Explanation**

Notice that to declare an infinite for loop, you just need to have two semicolons in the parentheses associated with the for keyword, that is:

```
for(;;){
  //this code will run infinitely
}
```

# Exercise

1. Rewrite the following loops as for loops.

a.

```
int x = 2;
while(x <= 200)
{
```

```
        if (x < 10 && x != 1)
        cout << 'YY';
        x=x+2;
}
```
b.
```
int a = 2;
while(a <=21)
{
        cout << 'YY';
        a++;
}
```

2. What is the output of the following (when embedded in a complete program)?

```
for (int ctr = 2; ctr < 15; ctr++)
        cout << (3 + ctr) << endl;
```

3. What is the output of the following?

```
        for (int b = 50; b > 2; b = b - 3)
        {
                cout << "Hi ";
                cout << b << endl;
        }
```

4. Write a program that create prints out your name an infinite number of times using a for loop.

# Arrays

An array is a collection of values of the same data type.

Each value in the collection has an index associated with it that can be used to retrieve the value.

Indices in C++ start from 0 not 1, this is known as **zero based indexing.** It is like starting to count from 0 and not 1.

## Exercise

How many items do I have, if I gave them labels from 0 to 4?

Answer: 5

## Declaring an array

When declaring an array, we begin by specifying the data type of the values that the array will hold followed by the variable name of the array then by the number of elements it will hold in square brackets.

For example:

```
int size[4];
size = {1,2,3,4};
```

## Explanation

Above we have declared an array with the variable name *size* which holds 4 values of the data type integer

    int size[4];

    int -> data type of elements held by the array
    size -> name of the array
    [4] -> specification of the number of elements held by the array

The statement, size = {1, 2, 3, 4}, initializes an array, which simply means assigning a value to the array variable.

You can also declare and initialize an array at the same time as shown below:

## Example

int size[4] = { 1,2,3,4};
int size[] = { 1,2,3,4};

If the arguments are less, the rest are initialized to the zero value of the data type.

# Retrieving values from an array

Values are retrieved from an array by specifying the location of the needed value using an index

## Example

Let's say we want to retrieve the first element in an array, our code would be:

```cpp
#include<iostream>
using namespace std;

int main(){
    int size[4] = { 1,2,3,4};
    int firstElement = size[0];

    cout << firstElement ;
    return 0;
}
```

## Explanation

The line, int firstElement = size[0]; , retrieves the first element in the array.

Notice that since in C++ we start counting from 0, the index of the first element in the array is 0.
The program prints out 1 since the 1st element in size is 1.

# Exercise

Retrieve the fourth element. (Hint the index is not 4)

# Looping through elements in an array

If we want to retrieve all the elements in an array, we can use loops to do that.
We will use *for* loop since it is the simplest way to go about it.

# Example

```
main.cpp X
 1    #include<iostream>
 2    using namespace std;
 3
 4    int main(){
 5        int size[4] = { 1,2,3,4};
 6
 7        for(int i = 0 ; i < 4; i++){
 8            cout << size[i] ;
 9        }
10        return 0;
11    }
```

## Explanation

Notice that we start our counter from 0 and our condition is that the value of the counter $i$ should be less than 4, which is the size of the array.

# Exercise

This is to be done in one file:

1. Write a function that calculates the area of a circle.
2. Create an array that holds 10 circle radii that you want to know the areas of.
3. Loop through the array to calculate the areas of the circles and print the result to the screen
4. Calculate only the area of the circle in the fourth position in the array.
5. Create an array of the character of your name and print all of the characters to the screen.

# Structures

A structure is a group of values that enables you to order data in a logical manner, that is, in a manner that makes sense to you.

Let's say that you want to collect information about your friends' age, weight and height.

With the current knowledge we have we would do it something like this:

## Example code

```
main.cpp  X

1      #include<iostream>
2      using namespace std;
3
4      int main(){
5          int kevinAge = 10;
6          int kevinWeight = 30;
7          int kevinHeight = 1;
8
9          int jesiccaAge = 15;
10         int jesiccaWeight = 28;
11         int jesiccaHeight = 1;
12     }
13
```

Structures make grouping such information easier.

Let's first define a structure.

# Structure definition

```
main.cpp  ×
1        #include<iostream>
2        using namespace std;
3
4        struct PersonInfo{
5
6            int age;
7            int weight;
8            int height;
9        };
10
11       int main(){
12
13           return 0;
14       }
15
```

## Explanation

A structure is defined outside any function definition, including the main function.

We use the keyword **struct** to define a structure followed by the name we want to give the structure, this name is known as a *structure tag*

Inside the curly braces associated with the structure tag, we declare structure variables which are also known as *member names.* In the above example, **age**, **weight** and **height** are *member names.*

**Notice** that there is a semicolon after the closing curly brace.

# Initializing structures

```cpp
#include<iostream>
using namespace std;

struct PersonInfo{

    int age;
    int weight;
    int height;
};

int main(){

    // initializing the structure
    PersonInfo kevin = {10,30,1 };
    PersonInfo jesicca = {15,28,1 };

    return 0;
}
```

# Explanation

By creating a structure, we have created a new data type.

As we usually do when we declare any variables, we start with the data type that it will hold.

In curly braces we pass in the arguments to be values for the declared structure variables.

The order of the arguments is important.

You will get an error if there are more initializer values than structure members.

If the values are less, the last ones that aren't in the list are initialized to zero.

# Accessing struct member values

To access a structure's member variables value, you use the dot operator as shown below

Example code

```cpp
main.cpp X
1    #include<iostream>
2    using namespace std;
3
4    struct PersonInfo{
5
6        int age;
7        int weight;
8        int height;
9    };
10
11   int main(){
12
13       // initializing the structure
14       PersonInfo kevin = {10,30,1 };
15       PersonInfo jesicca = {15,28,1 };
16
17       cout << kevin.age << endl;
18       cout << jesicca.age << endl;
19
20       return 0;
21   }
```

The output for **kevin.age** and **jessica.age** are 10 and 15 in the output above. Age is the first member of the structure. 10 and 15 are the first numbers in the structure initialization, thus they reference Kevin and Jessica's age.

# Exercise

Create a structure called Date, that has the member variables year, month and day. Initialize it with your current date and print all the values to the screen.

# Final Project

In the final project, we aim to utlize a lot of the skills we've learned throughout the book.

## Tasks

Design a student management system. New students are added with information entered including their name and registration number. The user can search the particular student on the basis of registration number. The user can check the entire list of students and delete a particular student in the basis of registration number and exit the program.

The code below performs the task; and all the tasks are explained clearly after the program.

# Code

```cpp
#include<iostream>    |
using namespace std;
#include <string>

// search record function to search the record of the student if it is exist and then print record
void searchRecord(string name[], string regnum[], string reg,int in) {

    // is found variable to check wether a record is exist or not in the array if exist set it true
    bool isfound = false;

        // loop till array to check a wether a record exist or not
        for(int index = 0; index < in; index = index + 1) {

            // check the every record in array if match then
            if ( regnum[index] == reg ) {

                // record is found
                isfound = true;

                // printing the record
                cout << "Student Registration Number  :   "
                << regnum[index]    << "\t\t" <<   " Student Name : "   << name[index] << endl;
                cout << endl;



                // terminating from loop
                break;

            }
        }

        // if a particular record is not exist then
        if (isfound == false) {

            // display that record is not exist
            cout <<" Record is not found : " <<endl;
            cout << endl;
        }
    }

int  main()
{
    // loop control variable set it true when the user exist from the programme set cont false
    bool cont = true;

    // registration number array to store the user registration number
    string registrationNum[100];
    |
```

```cpp
// student name array to store the student registration number
string name[100];

// declaring variable to store the user entered option
int selectedNumber;

// indext to count the total number of added student
int index = 0;

// loop till user exit the programme
while(cont) {

    // printing menu
    cout << "[1] Create New Record \n"
    <<"[2] Search A Record \n[3] View All Record \n[4] Delete a Record \n[5] Exit  \n"<<endl;

    // prompt user to enter the number
    cout << "Select Number : ";

    // store the user entered number in selectedNumber
    cin >> selectedNumber;

    // if the selectedNumber is 1 then add record into array


    if ( selectedNumber == 1) {

        // declare nam and regNum variable to store the user entered nam and regNum
        string nam;
        string regNum;

        // prompt user to enter name
        cout << "Enter your name : ";

        // store the user enter name into nam variable
        cin >> nam;

        //prompt user to enter the registration number
        cout << "Enter your Registration Number : ";
        cin >> regNum;

        // storing the user entered name and regNum into their respective array
        registrationNum[index] = regNum;
        name[index] = nam;

        // incrementing index
        index = index + 1;
        cout << endl;
```

```cpp
}

// check if user entered 2 then
else if ( selectedNumber == 2)
{

    // check if there is at least one record in the array then
    if ( index >= 0) {

        // prompt user to enter registration number
        string renum;
        cout << "Enter Your Registration Number :";

        // storing the user entered registration number into renum variable
        cin >> renum;

        // calling the function which fine a record and print it
        searchRecord(name,registrationNum,renum,index);

    }


    // if there is no record in the array then




    else {

        // simply print there is no record in the system
        cout << "There is no Record In the System" <<endl;
        cout << endl;
    }
}

// check if the user entered number 3 then
else if ( selectedNumber == 3 ) {

    // Printing all the records of students
    for (int i = 0; i < index; i++) {

        // if there is null in the array which record is deleted
        if ( name[i] == "null" )
        {
            // just ignore that index
            continue;
        }

        else {
            |
```

```cpp
            // printing all the record of student
            cout << "Student Registration Number  :  " <<  registrationNum[i]   <<
            "\t\t" <<   " Student Name :  "  << name[i] << endl;
        }

    }

    // adding space
    cout << endl;

}

// check if the user entered the number 4 then
else if ( selectedNumber == 4 ) {

    // check there is any record in the array then
    if ( index >= 0) {

        // declare the variable renum to store the user registartion number
        string renum;

        // prompt user to enter registration number
        cout << "Enter Your Registration Number :";
        cin >> renum;


        // is found variable which check if the record is found or not in array
        bool isfound = false;

        // loop till the end of number of record
        for(int ind = 0; ind < index; ind = ind + 1 ){

            // check if the user entered registration is equal to registration num in array
            if ( registrationNum[ind] == renum ) {

                // set the value of found to true
                isfound = true;

                // adding the null to arrays where value is found
                name[ind] = "null";
                registrationNum[ind] = "null";

                // just print that record deleted successfully
                cout << " Record deleted successfully : " <<endl;
                cout << endl;
            }

        }

    // if the user entered registration number is not found then
```

```cpp
        if (isfound == false) {

            // print record id not found
            cout <<" Record is not found : " <<endl;
            cout << endl;

        }
    }

    // if there is no record in the array then
    else {

        // print record is not exits
        cout <<" There is no record in the system: " <<endl;
        cout << endl;
    }

}

// check if the user entered the number 5 then
else if( selectedNumber == 5 ) {

    // print take care
     cout <<" Take Care " <<endl;



    // set cont to flase so that programme terminate
    cont = false;

}

else {

    // if the user did not enter any number from 1-5 then print please enter valid number
    cout <<" Invalid entry : " <<endl;
    cout << endl;
    }
}
    return 0;

}
```

```
[1] Create New Record
[2] Search A Record
[3] View All Record
[4] Delete a Record
[5] Exit

Select Number : 1
Enter your name : john
Enter your Registration Number : 44

[1] Create New Record
[2] Search A Record
[3] View All Record
[4] Delete a Record
[5] Exit

Select Number : 1
Enter your name : jimmy
Enter your Registration Number : 66

[1] Create New Record
[2] Search A Record
[3] View All Record
[4] Delete a Record
[5] Exit

Select Number : 1
Enter your name : hussain
Enter your Registration Number : 12

[1] Create New Record
[2] Search A Record
[3] View All Record
[4] Delete a Record
[5] Exit

Select Number : 2
Enter Your Registration Number :12
Student Registration Number  :  12                    Student Name : hussain
```

```
[1] Create New Record
[2] Search A Record
[3] View All Record
[4] Delete a Record
[5] Exit

Select Number : 3
Student Registration Number  :  44            Student Name : john
Student Registration Number  :  66            Student Name : jimmy
Student Registration Number  :  12            Student Name : hussain

[1] Create New Record
[2] Search A Record
[3] View All Record
[4] Delete a Record
[5] Exit

Select Number : 4
Enter Your Registration Number :66
 Record deleted successfully :
```

```
[1] Create New Record
[2] Search A Record
[3] View All Record
[4] Delete a Record
[5] Exit

Select Number : 3
Student Registration Number  :  44            Student Name : john
Student Registration Number  :  12            Student Name : hussain

[1] Create New Record
[2] Search A Record
[3] View All Record
[4] Delete a Record
[5] Exit

Select Number : 5
 Take Care

-----------------------------------
Process exited after 40.77 seconds with return value 0
Press any key to continue . . .
```

# Add a record in array

We have declared two arrays for student names and student registration numbers. The two arrays are called **registrationNum** and **nam**.

If the user enters the number '1' then program will ask user to enter student name and registration number. The user then enters the name and registration number. It is stored in their respective array. There is count variable called **index** which counts the number of students which are created. The index is increased by 1 each time a student is added. The process of adding the record is shown in the part of the code below.

```
if ( selectedNumber == 1) {

    // declare nam and regNum variable to store the user entered nam and regNum
    string nam;
    string regNum;

    // prompt user to enter name
    cout << "Enter your name : ";

    // store the user enter name into nam variable
    cin >> nam;

    //prompt user to enter the registration number
    cout << "Enter your Registration Number : ";
    cin >> regNum;

    // storing the user entered name and regNum into their respective array
    registrationNum[index] = regNum;
    name[index] = nam;

    // incrementing index
    index = index + 1;
    cout << endl;
```

# Search record from the array

A user can search a particular student using their enrolled registration number by pressing '2' at the start of the program.
The program first checks if the student array is empty. If the array is not empty, the user then enters the registration number. The program compares the user-entered registration with registration numbers existing in array. It does this using the function *searchRecord()*.

```
}
// check if user entered 2 then
else if ( selectedNumber == 2)
{

    // check if there is at least one record in the array then
    if ( index >= 0) {

        // prompt user to enter registration number
        string renum;
        cout << "Enter Your Registration Number :";

        // storing the user entered registration number into renum variable
        cin >> renum;

        // calling the function which fine a record and print it
        searchRecord(name,registrationNum,renum,index);

    }

    // if there is no record in the array then
```

The function **searchRecord()** takes in an array of names **(name[])** and an array of registration numbers **(regnum[])** as arguments. It also takes in two variables for registration number **reg** and index **in**.

**reg** is the registration number we are using to search for the student record, while **in** is the number of records.

The function search the array **regum[]** using a for loop for the registration number **reg**.

If **reg** is found, the function prints out the student registration number and name.

If **reg** is not found, the function prints out "Record is not found"

```
// search record function to search the record of the student if it is exist and then print record
void searchRecord(string name[], string regnum[], string reg,int in) {

    // is found variable to check wether a record is exist or not in the array if exist set it true
    bool isfound = false;

    // loop till array to check a wether a record exist or not
    for(int index = 0; index < in; index = index + 1) {

        // check the every record in array if match then
        if ( regnum[index] == reg ) {

            // record is found
            isfound = true;

            // printing the record
            cout << "Student Registration Number  :  "
                 << regnum[index]   << "\t\t" <<  " Student Name : " << name[index] << endl;
            cout << endl;



            // terminating from loop
            break;
        }
    }

    // if a particular record is not exist then
    if (isfound == false) {

        // display that record is not exist
        cout <<" Record is not found : " <<endl;
        cout << endl;
    }
}
```

# View all the records

To view all the record of students, the user presses '3' at the start of the program. There is count variable called *index* which count the number of students. A for loop is used to retrieve each student record and print out each student name and registration number. The loop continues till it reaches the value of *index* which indicates that we are at the end of the array.

```cpp
// check if the user entered number 3 then
else if ( selectedNumber == 3 ) {

    // Printing all the records of students
    for (int i = 0; i < index; i++) {

        // if there is null in the array which record is deleted
        if ( name[i] == "null" )
        {
            // just ignore that index
            continue;
        }

        else {
            |

            // printing all the record of student
            cout << "Student Registration Number  :  " <<  registrationNum[i]   <<
            "\t\t" <<  " Student Name : "   << name[i] << endl;
        }

    }
    // adding space
    cout << endl;

}
```

# Delete a record

If the user presses '4' at the start of the program, the user can delete a particular student on the basis of registration number.
The user first enters the registration number into a variable called *renum*. The program will check if student array is empty then display there is no record in the system if it is empty. If the array is not empty then the program compares the *renum* with registration numbers which

are in array ***registrationNum***. This is done using a for loop that iterates through the array. If the student is found then the record is deleted from the array by declaring the relevant name and registrationNum to null.

If the student record is not found then the program prints "Record is not found".

```cpp
// check if the user entered the number 4 then
else if ( selectedNumber == 4 ) {

    // check there is any record in the array then
    if ( index >= 0) {

        // declare the variable renum to store the user registartion number
        string renum;

        // prompt user to enter registration number
        cout << "Enter Your Registration Number :";
        cin >> renum;
        // is found variable which check if the record is found or not in array
        bool isfound = false;

        // loop till the end of number of record
        for(int ind = 0; ind < index; ind = ind + 1 ){

            // check if the user entered registration is equal to registration num in array
            if ( registrationNum[ind] == renum ) {

                // set the value of found to true
                isfound = true;

                // adding the null to arrays where value is found
                name[ind] = "null";
                registrationNum[ind] = "null";

                // just print that record deleted successfully
                cout << " Record deleted successfully : " <<endl;
                cout << endl;
            }

        }

    // if the user entered registration number is not found then

    // if there is no record in the array then
    else {

        // print record is not exits
        cout <<" There is no record in the system: " <<endl;
        cout << endl;
    }

}
```

# Exit

If the user enter the number '5' then simply break from the loop. The variable **cont** is set to false. This terminates the program as the program is in a while loop that continues while **cont** is true.

```cpp
// check if the user entered the number 5 then
else if( selectedNumber == 5 ) {

    // print take care
    cout <<" Take Care " <<endl;

    // set cont to flase so that programme terminate
    cont = false;

}
```

www.ingramcontent.com/pod-product-compliance
Ingram Content Group UK Ltd.
Pitfield, Milton Keynes, MK11 3LW, UK
UKHW021325020125
3930UKWH00043B/488

9 781922 659231